STRAIGHT UP

FINDING COURAGE
TO BE A MAN

MICHAEL DAVIS JR.

Straight Up! Finding Courage to be a Man
by Michael Davis Jr.

Published by HigherLife Development Services, Inc.
400 Fontana Circle
Building 1—Suite 105
Oviedo, Florida 32765
(407) 563-4806
www.ahigherlife.com

Unless otherwise indicated, Bible quotations are taken from the King James Version.

ISBN 13: 978-1-939183-08-8
ISBN 10: 1939183081

Cover Design: Dave Whitlock
First Edition12 13 14 15 — 9 8 7 6 5 4 3 2 1

ACKNOWLEDGEMENTS

I'd like to thank my Lord Jesus for dying on the cross for my sins!

To my wife Fredricka, thank you for everything you do, it would take many more pages to list all that you do! I love you.

I'd like to thank my sons, Michael and Kyle, for being the greatest sons a father could ask for! You are a great inspiration to me! Go after your dreams, God can make them happen!

To my mother, thank you for being there for me and providing for our family in the midst of the concrete jungle! To my sisters, thank you for always being there!

To my boy Jay, thanks for always having my back and I appreciate all the counsel!

Thanks to Bishop Butler & the entire Word of Faith Family for teaching me the Word of God!

And thanks to all the friends and family members who have had an impact on my life!

TABLE OF CONTENTS

INTRODUCTION

Growing up in Detroit Michigan, we had our fair share of challenges. Add to those challenges poverty, violence, and being raised in a single parent household. My father lived in the same city, but was absent physically and financially. My mother, on welfare at the time, did a tremendous job raising my sister and me.

I always dreamed of having a close relationship with my father, but that would never happen. And as I grew older, I noticed that some of my peers were receiving wisdom from their fathers that I was missing out on.

God began to put replacement men in my life that helped fill the void my father had left. As I began to seek God, He began to provide me with the wisdom I sought.

This book is written to young men who are willing to learn from the blessings and mistakes of others. I have written in parables or short stories to relate God's Word with real life situations. Stories that can be read alone, father and son teams or single mother son teams can read them together. This can also be read in a group setting.

Prayerfully, this book will help you miss some of the pot holes and land mines set across your path. My hope is that this book will foster healthy communication between you and your parents or mentors, which will create close, long lasting bonds. This, in turn, will give you the love you are desperately seeking in less positive avenues, and set you on the path of greatness!

APPETITE: TAME THE BEAST WITHIN

Tame the beast called appetite
Once he's captured your mind, brace for a fight.
Gain control before it gets out of hand.
Whole foods are what your body demands.

Larry would often eat processed foods and plenty of sweets. He craved those foods. Although he had been warned to slow down, he continued eating the white bread, white rice, and white pasta. When his blood sugar level surpassed the 500 mark, he had to be rushed to the hospital. They had to give him insulin intravenously. The doctors informed Larry that, due to the constant spiking of his blood sugar level, his pancreas had stopped secreting insulin, so they were giving him insulin to get his blood sugar level back to normal. They also informed him that if he didn't change his diet, he could lose his vision and maybe have limbs amputated. His appetite had to be disciplined immediately!

Larry changed his diet – eating more fruits and vegetables. He ate brown rice, whole wheat bread, and wheat pastas instead of the white counterpart. His doctors told him that when eating the white pastas and white breads, it was like eating sugar because of how fast it turned to sugar when it hit his tongue. He drank plenty of water instead of soda pop or juices. Eventually, his blood sugar level was normal and his doctor was able to remove him from the insulin.

Food should be fuel for our bodies. But if our appetite is out of control, food can be our worst enemy. Consistently eating too much of the wrong foods can cause sickness and disease.

Inform yourself on what's inside the food you are eating. Read the labels. Get an understanding of the ingredients. Learn the nutritional terms. Our bodies are the temple of the Holy Spirit. Treat your body as if God is living on the inside of you—because He is!

PROVERBS 23:2 (THE MESSAGE)
And don't stuff yourself, bridle your appetite.

GET YOURSELF TOGETHER FIRST

Females can wait; don't let them nab your heart.
Find God's purpose for your life and set out to hit your mark.
Emotional attachments will only send you on a long detour.
Like a pitcher of water, tilt your heart, and into His hands start to pour.

While in college, Marty had a long distance relationship with his girlfriend. He felt like he was in love with her. She got pregnant and eventually had a baby. The baby girl was named after Marty and he became attached to her. After about four months, Marty was told that the baby was not his child. Hurt and angry, Marty didn't know what to do; he felt lost. His girlfriend even claimed that she was raped by a guy Marty played basketball with.

So Marty was confused. Should he leave her? Should he stay? Should he hurt the guy who did this? He eventually had a man to man talk with the guy accused of the rape. The man revealed that it was not rape, but the two secretly had an affair. Marty then had a DNA test done, which cleared him from being the baby's father. He moved on – though hurt and full of baggage from this situation. Marty had lost his focus in college, which was to get an education.

Actually, the break up was the best thing that happened to Marty. With this girl out of the picture, he could regain his focus. He was too young to be involved in a serious relationship. And he wasn't ready to be intimate and emotionally attached.

Take heed to the females who seek to trap you before you can be launched into the purpose God has for you. Some situations can lead you into the wilderness. Stay on the path God has for you. Sometimes, you may think you are chasing a female, but actually, they are corralling you into their own trap. Guard your heart. Don't give your strength to a woman.

PROVERBS 31:3 (AMPLIFIED BIBLE)

Give not your strength to {loose} women, nor your ways
to those who and that which ruin and destroy kings.

SET BACKS ARE GROWTH OPPORTUNITIES

A set back doesn't mean to fail
It's only failure when you permanently detour from the life trail.
Never stay down and you'll always have a chance.
Stay up so you have an opportunity to have that final dance.

Robert was a high school freshman. He skipped classes often, causing him to receive failing grades. Those poor grades delayed his desire to play basketball. A conversation with a senior teammate challenged him. The senior had earned a full scholarship to a local university. Hearing this motivated Robert so much that he set his mind to pursue a basketball scholarship.

Robert's grades began to soar from well below a 2.0 grade point average to well above a 3.0 grade point average. Robert diligently studied and practiced his basketball skills, and he earned a basketball scholarship to college.

Poor grades early in his high school career caused a temporary set back in fulfilling his dream. But a change in his thinking changed the course of his life. One conversation caused Robert to change the course of his life. With the scholarship as his vision, he set out to achieve greater marks in school and worked extremely hard on his basketball skills. It wasn't too late for Robert to change and it's not too late for anyone to change!

When you find yourself flat on your back from one of life's fierce blows, always get back up! The only way you lose is to stay down. Get up as fast as you can. There are some people that have gotten knocked down years ago and are still down. Life basically stopped at that set back. Storms are only temporary; the sun always comes out again.

PROVERBS 12:28

In the way of righteousness is life: and in the pathway thereof there is no death.

SHOW HIM RESPECT

This is not a fear that is afraid, but it is that of respect.
God sits on top, not to halt fun, just to protect.
God has barriers, like seatbelts, in place,
To keep us from falling flat on our face.

Corey was twenty-one years old, and while attending college, he had an epiphany. God began to touch his heart. He had been accustomed to drinking lots of alcohol at various parties. He also had slept with women whom he wasn't married to.

Suddenly, he realized he shouldn't sleep with females unless he was married to them. And the drinking just didn't feel right. He began to read the Quaran in his search to find God. Because he felt that Muslims catered more to African Americans, he decided to attend a Mosque in his city. They greeted him with love. They sat him on one side with all the other men, and the women were seated on the opposite side.

During the sermon, the preacher repeatedly stated that the white man was the devil —not some of them, but all of them. Corey knew that this way of thinking was wrong. Corey also knew that God did not have hatred for people. Corey, out of respect for God, wanted to do what was right. So, he left the Mosque and never returned. Corey continued his search for God and eventually gave his life to the Lord Jesus Christ! He still loved his Muslim brothers, but just preferred to follow the love of God.

When we respect God, we listen and follow what He says. When we respect God, we respect what He respects. So we obey God's commandments out of respect for Him. Even when we may not understand why, we just do it out of respect for Him. We love the brethren because God has said it. Or when God says respect our bodies as the home of where His Spirit dwells, we must watch what we consume in the form of food in respect of His Word. This respect is considered the fear of the Lord, the beginning of true knowledge.

PROVERBS 1:7

The fear of the Lord is the beginning of knowledge:
but fools despise wisdom and instruction.

GO WITH THE LIGHT

Keep God's commandment at the forefront of your mind.
It will light the path you walk, so the darkness isn't making you blind.
Insert light & it will reveal what's inside of a room.
Light illuminates any impending doom.

Brian was in school playing basketball on an athletic scholarship. Very athletic, he could jump out of the gym. His future was bright. Although his school was 3,000 miles away, he flew home often. His girlfriend worked at an airline company, which gave him access to airline tickets at a discount rate. When he returned to school, he would always have brand new gym shoes and fresh gear. He would also fill the refrigerator in their apartment with tons of food. On one occasion, he left as normal to visit his home town, but he never returned.

His roommates found that Brian had been selling drugs in his home town. One day, while he was making a drop and driving a stolen car, the police attempted to pull him over for a traffic stop. Brian fled and led the police on a chase through the neighborhood. What Brian didn't know is that two people were crossing the street just ahead. Unable to stop, Brian struck and killed both the people as they crossed the street.

Brian found himself facing two murder charges. Although he didn't intend to kill the two innocent people, the damage had been done. After the court proceedings, he went to prison for the two lives he took. Leaving the path of light and entering the path of darkness had a major impact on the next phase of Brian's life.

God's Word serves as a light when we obey Him. Detours away from God's path of light are like walking inside a house at night – where all power has been lost. The darker the path, the more you stumble and fall. Stay on God's well lit path. Avoid being deceived into exiting the path. It doesn't matter how attractive the detour appears; God's path is always the best!

PROVERBS 6:23
For the commandment is a lamp, and the law is light,
and reproofs of instruction are the way of life.

GOD IS OUR SOURCE

Set your heart to give to those in need.
Refuse to be a hoarder, adopt a mind set of sowing good seed.
Never allow your intentions to be anchored in greed.

Allen had just completed his master's degree. At this point, most people would want to find the highest paying job they could find. But, instead of seeking a new career or a great paying job to just make money, Allen followed an overwhelming desire in his heart to help the homeless.

Without a job or any income, he began living with the homeless, outside or wherever they lived. As God provided his financial need, Allen used the resources to buy food and meet the needs of the homeless. As Allen's resources increased, he gave more and more to the homeless. His genuine love for each person he came in contact with spread. He was welcomed and trusted in the circles of the homeless.

God eventually inspired a Good Samaritan to bless him with funding. Allen used this funding to purchase housing and transportation for the homeless. He had befriended the homeless individuals and now they had a place to live. Allen used the transportation he purchased to transport them to different employment opportunities they had received. As Allen continued to receive more donations, he created a nonprofit organization. Now he uses the organization to raise more funds to provide for the homeless. He is also able to pay himself a salary. When you take care of God's work, He will take care of you.

Always remember God is your source. Whatever job you may be working, it's just an assignment. If it expires, then God will give you a new assignment. You don't have to become a man pleaser to stay on an assignment. Do your best on every assignment for the glory of God! But you don't have to sell your soul so that man can extend favor toward you.

PROVERBS 13:7

There is that maketh himself rich, yet hath nothing:
there is that maketh himself poor, yet hath great riches.

THE DRUG GAME WON'T LAST

Increase gradually; stay clear of the desire to enter the fast lane.
Many seek fast money, by entering the drug game.
Follow God's process to get wealth.
It doesn't consist of moving fast, like a stealth.

Growing up in a poor neighborhood, Harold always wanted the finer things of life. He saw that the drug dealers had the things he wished he had. He saw they had the Starter jackets, the top tens, the big gold chains, the four finger rings, and the girls. These guys also had the fancy cars with the chrome wheels. Harold always admired the criminal lifestyle; he saw it as his way of coming up out of the ghetto. Going to school was never his thing. He actually viewed school as a place for suckers.

So Harold got into the drug game and money began to come in fast. He suddenly had stylish clothes, shoes, jewelry, and fancy cars. But as quickly as Harold rose in hood status, the jealousy of his haters rose. One day, in the middle of the afternoon while he was parked outside his mother's house, a masked gunman ran up to his truck and shot him multiple times in the face and head. Harold was gunned down at the age of twenty-five. A closed casket was required, due to the extensive gunshot wounds to his face.

There are no rules in this game. Anything goes!
There is no love in the Devil and no love in the games he funds!

The lifestyle may appear to be the way to go — on the outside looking in. What are the options? Death or prison. The Devil will love if you pick either one. If you are making money, your competition will not like it. They will seek to steal your money and your clientele. Going to the police doesn't always work because both sides might be on the wrong side of the law.

Remain faithful in the field God has placed you in. Increase gradually. As you remain faithful in one area, allow God to promote you as you're ready.

PROVERBS 20:12

An inheritance may be gotten hastily at the beginning;
but the end thereof shall not be blessed.

EVERY CHOICE BUILDS TOWARD A GOOD NAME

When life presents situations outside your picture frame,
before responding, remember the importance of a good name.
The habit of lying today will make you a liar tomorrow
And when loved ones doubt your word,
it brings you great sorrow.

Judas was one of the twelve disciples Jesus chose. Once chosen, Judas was around Jesus quite often. While Jesus taught all the lessons and the Holy Spirit descended on Him, Judas was there. But instead of allowing the Words of Jesus to get into his heart, he allowed greed to enter into his heart and suffocate the Word. Once the seed of greed was planted into his heart, the enemy launched at the opportunity to use Judas to help destroy Jesus. Judas was offered thirty pieces of silver to betray Jesus. Because Judas had opened a door for the Devil to enter, he gladly accepted the offer. His name was marked that day. The series of choices Judas made ultimately led to his downfall. If he had made different choices, his name could be known as something more positive. But, instead, Judas immediately went from a disciple to being a traitor. And from that day forward, the name Judas is synonymous with being a traitor, not as a disciple of Jesus.

The choices and decisions we make on a daily basis play a part in developing a good or a bad name. Make wise decisions to maintain a good name for you and all the other people that came before you. You will be judged based on your past reputation. Your family will be affected by the decisions you make. If you're approaching graduation, your parent's coworkers are also inquiring about your pending graduation. And your parents are either proud or ashamed, depending on whether you are taking care of your business.

PROVERBS 22:7

A good name is rather to be chosen than great riches,
and loving favour rather than silver and gold.

STAY IN YOUR LANE

There is a lane that God has especially designed for you.
Following the path of another just won't do.
On this path is where your blessings lie.
You won't find them on another person's path,
no matter how hard you try.

Curtis worked at a fast food restaurant earning minimum wage, but dreamed of one day investing in real estate. Armed with a vision of owning multiple real estate investment properties, Curtis began saving his money. He viewed a duplex that was for sale at a price he believed was reachable. Curtis hadn't changed jobs or made any extra money, but he was filled with joy. The joy came from the vision that had engulfed his heart. When his feet hit the floor each morning, he had the vision of purchasing this duplex at the forefront of his mind. Finally, Curtis saved enough money to purchase the duplex. Curtis made an offer on the duplex and they accepted it. After repairing the duplex, Curtis moved into one side and leased out the other side. The rent he received from his tenant paid for his expenses, so he was able to continue to save. After some time, Curtis bought another duplex, leased out both sides of the first duplex, and also leased out one side of his new duplex. Curtis was well on his way to seeing his vision come to pass!

God has planted certain qualities and talents inside of each of us. Find what talents He has placed inside of you. The gifts inside you must be nurtured and brought from inside and made into a reality. Don't get side tracked away from these gifts inside you. And don't let your motives just be money or fame. If you go after money or fame, you will be miserable and out of God's will for your life. Even if it appears that your path may not pay a whole lot of money, follow the path anyway. Stay in this lane; it is the best place for you!

PROVERBS 4:18

But the path of the just is as the shining light, that shineth
more and more unto the perfect day.

THE POINT OF NO RETURN

A wise man will turn away from wrath.
A calm man or an angry man, which will cause more trouble?
You do the math!
Learn to calm the inner man that when angered will arise.
Learn what triggers your anger; don't let it be a surprise.

Dan was 40 years old, working as a foreman at Ford Motor Company. One day, he was at his relative's house for a family gathering. His nephew was there and began mouthing off at his uncle Dan. Dan brushed it off at first, but became increasingly angered by his nephew's comments. Eventually, the exchange between the two came to the point of arguing and the two went face to face. The confrontation escalated to the point that Dan pulled his 45 caliber from his waist band and fired two shots into the stomach of his nephew. Dan was arrested. During the booking process at the police station, he spoke with the officer finger-printing him. The officer asked, "Couldn't you have settled the dispute with your nephew in a better way than shooting him?" Dan responded, "I'm tired of that nigga coming around here trying to act hard!" A few moments later, Dan began to come down from his rage. He said, "What have I done? I'm a man of God!" Dan had given in to the rage he felt and would have to suffer massive consequences for his actions. As Dan cried, he realized that the Devil had used him for his work.

CAUTION, Anger is often used to detour you away from the path of life. When a person is calm, it is much more difficult to lure them away. But when a person is angry, they are more likely to do things they normally wouldn't do. Many people have been murdered because their anger turned into wrath. When you're angry, learn to pause before reacting. This will allow you time to think it out first. You can't control what other people do, but you can work on controlling how you respond.

PROVERBS 16:32

He that is slow to anger is better than the mighty; and
he that ruleth his spirit than he that taketh a city.

GROWTH IS IN HEARING

Growth occurs when God's voice is clear.
Obey His words, trust Him without fear.
When you seek to avoid all forms of pain,
In your present state is where you'll remain.

Doug worked every day, but still had no money. One day, as he made out a check for his car note, he thought to himself, "I don't have any money!" God responded to him and said, "Add up the amount of the check." Doug grabbed a calculator and added up his car note amount by the number of months of his lease. As he starred at this figure on his calculator, God said, "There is your extra money!" God went on to show him that by leasing this borrowed vehicle for $16,000 over three years, he would return the vehicle when the lease was completed. Doug heard God speak to him. Once Doug's lease was done, he began paying himself the amount he paid the financing company. He didn't renew the lease. He didn't sign a contract for a new lease. Instead, he bought a nice used car. He distanced himself from the mindset of leasing a brand new car every two years.

Listen for God's voice early and always! Before making any moves, seek Him first. Resist the temptation to do it alone. God's view from the top shines light on the dark corners hidden from our sight. A Word from God will change the course of your life, just one Word! God's Word can take you from poor to rich, sad to glad, sick to healthy!

PROVERBS 1:5

A wise man will hear, and will increase learning; and a man of understanding shall attain unto wise counsels:

PAY CASH AS MUCH AS POSSIBLE

Following this world system will lead you down a
path loaded with debt.
As much as possible, stay away from purchasing items on credit.
If you become enslaved by debt, it's never too late to shed it.

Maceo had a family of three and his wife was pregnant. They had a mortgage and his wife's car note was still outstanding. Maceo's lease on his pick-up truck had just recently expired and he purchased a used car. Maceo's wife was ordered, by her physician, to stop working. As Maceo was beginning to feel the pressure of being the man of his household, God spoke a Word to him. He told him to begin to pay all their bills with his check, and to save every one of his wife's checks as if they were nonexistent. God told him to do this during the six months that his wife would be off of work. Maceo thought, "How is this going to work?" He figured he didn't make enough money to pay all their bills with his check alone. But Maceo obeyed the voice of God and began to implement the plan God had given him. When the period ended, Maceo had accumulated enough to pay the remaining balance on his wife's car. From that day forward, Maceo tried to pay cash for anything he bought.

As much as possible when making purchases, pay them in full. It is a good policy to only purchase items that you can pay off completely. Don't form a mindset that it's OKAY to use credit now and pay the creditor later with interest. Save your money and when you obtain a cushion, make smaller purchases while you continue to stack money.

PROVERBS 22:7

The rich ruleth over the poor, and the borrower is
servant to the lender.

12

ESTABLISH YOUR LIFE FIRST

Before building a family, know God's will for your life for sure.
Building a home for them to move into is a serious chore.
Write your vision and follow God's leading.
Learn to follow before you consider leading.

Thomas was 18 years old and just graduated from High School. His parents had always planned for him to go straight to college, but Thomas was in love with his girlfriend. He was working at a temporary service and figured he'd continue working this job, holding off on going to college. Thomas really hadn't taken the time to seek God for his purpose in life. His girlfriend got pregnant and neither one of them had acquired a trade or any skills. Thomas struggled to make ends meet even with the addition of another part time job. He was totally frustrated as he and his family lived with his mother in a small room in the basement. Thomas never went to college or acquired any skills for the job market. The relationship with his girl faded as the money issue caused a rift between the two of them. She ended up with another guy, and sought child support from Thomas, which only added to his money woes.

Find out what God's plan is for your life first. Learn how to cook, clean, and do laundry for yourself. Establish your home. Purchase your car. Become very comfortable being single. When these things are established, and when the time is right, allow God to lead you in marrying your wife. And once God leads you in choosing a mate, enjoy her for some time before having children.

PROVERBS 24:27

Prepare thy work without, and make it fit for thyself in the field; and afterwards build thine house.

WHEN YOU LAY, MAKE SURE IT'S WHERE YOU STAY

One way to keep your finances in your home,
is to raise your children under one roof with the
wife of your youth alone.
With your wife is where you lay.
With your wife and kids is where you stay.

Maurice was young and felt it was OKAY to hook up with Jennifer without a jimmy hat. They weren't married, but everyone was doing it, so Maurice followed suit. Maurice never considered Lisa to be the marriage type, but was infatuated with her body and her looks. He continued the relationship with her and they ultimately had two children, but their relationship failed. Later, Maurice found the woman of his dreams and married her. Maurice worked hard, but his baby's mama, Lisa, demanded that she be paid child support for their two children. After the child support payments were deducted from his check every week, he didn't have enough money to live off of. His money landed in the house of another house hold every week when his child support was deducted from his check. This past baggage was having an impact on his current relationship. His baby's mama had become involved in another relationship and Maurice's child support checks funded her new household. Because this money was deducted from each one of his checks, Maurice struggled in his current relationship.

When you seek to date a girl, only date a woman for the purpose of deciding if she will possibly become your wife one day. Don't date for any other reason. Get to know the woman and avoid becoming attached emotionally to her. If you don't test the water, you won't have children out of wedlock. And your income will remain in your household; it won't be scattered to multiple households.

PROVERBS 5:10

Lest strangers be filled with thy wealth; and thy
labours be in the house of a stranger.

DO THE RIGHT THING

Behave with good judgment even if it appears no one is around.
God has eyes and ears all over to help keep our character sound.
Within us is where His Spirit lies.
He will lead us to the ultimate prize.

Devon had a secret. He enjoyed stealing things that didn't belong to him. It seems that he had gotten away with stealing several times before. He felt that he was pretty good at it. He was not stealing because of a need. It felt sort of like a sport because of the adrenaline rush each time he got away with it.

One day, Devon entered a department store and placed several items down his pants. He began walking toward the front door, feeling pretty good about himself, but this time was different. As he pushed the door to exit, a security guard grabbed his arm and said, "Come with me!" The security guard took Devon to the back of the store and showed him a video. The video showed the entire incident. Devon watched the video and saw himself taking their product from the shelf and shoving it inside his pants. Devon felt awful and vowed to never do it again! The security guard extended mercy to Devon by not calling the police, but told Devon that he would be banned from the store for six months, and posted his picture on the store bulletin board. His photo remained in the store for six months and the caption underneath his photo read, "Banned from this store!"

God is always watching! Rules and laws are in place for our protection, not for God to lord over us as the judge. Even though He is! Get in the habit of doing the right thing. Whether you think someone is watching or not, there is always a way of finding out a wrong that has been committed.

PROVERBS 6:20-21

My son, keep thy father's commandment, and forsake
not the law of thy mother: Bind them continually upon
thine heart, and tie them about thy neck.

SPEAK ABOUT THE GOOD GOD HAS DONE

Complaining may appear harmless in our eyes,
but God views it as the beginning of our demise.
There is always someone that is worse.
Things can always improve, as long as you're not
being carried away in a hearse.

As a pastor lay in bed, God asked him what he would do if he lost all his partners. The pastor began to think about all the things God had done for him. He thought about the fact that his plane was paid for, the hanger that it sat in was paid for, houses and cars were all paid for, God had showed him where to dig for natural gas, his water wells and purification systems were all paid for, and he had been debt free for over 40 years. He jumped out of bed so not to wake up his wife. And began to thank God for everything He had done. He was overjoyed by the way God had blessed him. And God had showed him that he wasn't dependent on the world's system for anything; God is his source.

There is always something to be grateful for. Whether things are going well or not, we should always always find something to be grateful for. Whatever you are ungrateful for, you are in danger of losing. Complaining is viewed as a bad thing in the eyes of God. Even a natural father doesn't like complaining. He wants to know that his children are grateful for what he has done for them. When his children are grateful, there is no limit to what he will do for them.

PROVERBS 10:32 (THE MESSAGE)
The lips of the godly speak helpful words, but the
mouth of the wicked speaks perverse words.

NO FAVORITISM WITH GOD

You will never have to go above who you are with God.
Being you is good enough; God will give you the nod.
God doesn't have favorites in His Fam.
Come to Him when everything is cool
or when you find yourself in a jam.

Slaves were treated badly by slave owners. I read a story once about a slave who was an extremely hard worker in the field of welding. He worked harder than anyone in his area. The key difference is that he didn't get paid for his services. One day, the slave owner promised him his freedom papers if he would work hard on a special project for three months. So he worked and worked each day with the thought of freedom on his mind. When the three months were over, the slave owner had sold the slave to a new slave owner. The new slave owner had no intention of honoring the agreement he had entered into with the former slave owner. This left the slave back in the hopeless situation he started out in before the agreement.

In the slave era, slaves were treated as animals at times. They had to eat anything that the slave owner didn't want to eat. And if they tried to escape, it was very difficult because of their skin color. If someone saw them, they knew that blacks were slaves. If an escape by a slave was unsuccessful, the slave owner would brand them with a hot iron with some sort of identifying mark. They even slept in very bad conditions. There was a distinct difference between whites and blacks.

God doesn't play favoritism with His children. What He does for one child, He will do for another child. Obedience is what God is searching for. Things like skin color, height, weight, background, upbringing, etc. are not in the equation between God and His children. Shoot for the stars. Ignore the people who speak negatively about your dream. When people say no, remember God says all things are possible to those who believe!

PROVERBS 24:23

These things also belong to the wise. It is not good to
have respect of persons in judgment.

DON'T BE ENTICED BY SINNERS

When you hang with sinners and they are doing wrong.
Death could show up singing your song.
Remember there are always consequences.
The choices you make can change your life in an instance.

Larry wanted to hang out with a group of guys who sold drugs to make money. This group of guys sold drugs from a woman addicted to crack cocaine. These guys gave her drugs or money to sell drugs from her house. One day, Larry decided that because he hadn't found a job for the summer yet, he would hang out with these guys inside the drug house. The guys mainly sat around playing video games, watching videos, drinking beer, and eating fast food. These actions were only interrupted when customers would walk up through the alley to the back of the house to buy drugs. The customers would say how many rocks they wanted to buy. They would exchange the money and the drugs through a small hole in the back of the house.

One night, there was a loud bang at the front door of this drug house. And before the guys could reach for their weapons, a masked gunman barged into the house armed with a sawed off shotgun. The spark from the blast of the shotgun was all that could be seen in the midst of the dark room. The guys began running towards the back of the house, as the masked gunman continued firing shotgun blasts their way. In a desperate escape for their lives, the guys jumped through the rear windows. The masked gunman then made off with all their drugs, money, and weapons. By the grace of God, this incident occurred a couple of days after Larry decided to hang out in this drug house.

Hanging out with people engaged in illegal activities can come back to haunt you. Even if you aren't physically participating in the illegal activity, remember, just being with the guys involved in the illegal activities can bring the same heat your way. When their enemies decide to seek revenge because of some past beef you know nothing about, the bullets will fly striking anyone in the area.

My son, if sinners entice thee consent thou not. If they say, come with us, let us lay wait for blood, let us lurk privily for the innocent without cause:

STOCK PILE EARLY AND OFTEN

Saving is a formidable habit one should learn.
How much you save is sometimes more important
than how much you earn.
Live below your means, so you can live comfortable
well past your teens.

Two childhood friends, raised in impoverished conditions, always dreamed of owning their own business. The problem was a lack of resources to start the business. The two friends began to save their money consistently. Saving money became a very enjoyable habit. They began to watch their money accumulate gradually. One day, an opportunity arose. A self-serve car wash was on the market for sale. As the two researched the self-serve car wash, they discovered that it was a cash business, their attendance wasn't always mandatory, the location of this one was in a prime location, and they had saved enough money to purchase it. They bought the car wash and continued working their jobs. This provided another stream of income. Although they had come from a poor neighborhood, they were able to save enough money to purchase the car wash. They had developed the habit of saving a portion of their income on a consistent basis. While running the business, their habit of saving continued to help them in their quest to run a successful business.

One day, they returned to their business to do the daily inspection and noticed that something was missing. The car wash had five vacuums. Each vacuum had a cover that was made of a valuable metal. The friends were unaware of this hot commodity. They found that in their area, individuals were stealing these metals and taking them to scrap metal businesses in the area that paid money for these metals. But because of their habit of saving, they were able to purchase new covers for the vacuum cleaners. This time they bought plastic covers.

Opportunities come to those who are prepared to take advantage when they present themselves. Prepare by laying aside some money. Emergencies will occur and if not prepared financially, these emergencies can leave you and your family homeless. Without savings, you are a slave to debt!

There is treasure to be desired and oil in the dwelling of the wise: but a foolish man spendeth it up.

LAZINESS IS CONTAGEOUS; KEEP AWAY!

Work as if you are working for the Lord.
Give one hundred percent effort every time,
God will take care of your reward.
Work hard even if you don't get the credit.
Be a doer of the Word because God said it.

Ronald grew up in a poor neighborhood in the inner city. But Ronald had two great parents in his household. His father worked as a foreman in the construction industry. He was also an entrepreneur; he created several businesses, which created many jobs for family and people in the neighborhood. His father was the one true man that many respected in the neighborhood. His father's integrity and strong work ethic brought a legacy for Ronald to follow. Ronald went on to earn his Bachelors degree, Masters Degree, and his P.h.D. He then worked as a White House Fellow, a Foreign Policy Advisor, served as an assistant to the President of Harvard University, the Chief Operating Officer & Executive Director of the Martin Luther King Jr. Center in Atlanta, GA; he served as Executive Director & President of the Congressional Black Caucus Foundation, along with many other companies and organizations. Ronald grabbed the baton from his father and extended the lead as he raced in the next leg of the race.

Hard work will definitely produce good results in your life. Complete tasks you don't want to complete early and often. If you only complete what you feel like doing, you will put yourself at a great disadvantage. Get up early and work late, for this life is short and many things need to be completed before you leave here!

PROVERBS 6:4

Give not sleep to thine eyes, nor slumber to thine eyelids.

A MENTOR FOR YOUR CRAFT

For your decisions to be sound, form yourself a circle of influence.
Listen to your mentor; remain in the front of class as he
speaks like "A" students.
A trusted person, whose advice is sound
Like twins attached to the hip is where you can be found.

The twelve disciples were blessed to have the Master Mentor. The disciples sat at the feet of Jesus daily. They watched as Jesus would go away for hours at a time and do this thing. They also noticed that when He would return from spending time doing this thing, He would return with power and demons would flee and people were healed. So one day, the disciples asked Jesus to teach them to pray. Jesus told them a story of a man who was asleep at home with his family one night. A friend came to his house requesting food, but the man refused to give him food. But Jesus said because of the friend's "importunity," which means shameless persistence, the man went and got his friend some food. Not because of their friendship. Jesus was basically saying this is how we should approach our prayer lives. Keep asking until we get what we came for! Because the disciples were with Jesus all the time, being mentored, they were able to receive these and many other life changing lessons.

Whatever craft or purpose you choose to pursue, you may hit a wall as far as going to the next level. You may only have limited knowledge in a certain area, but remember God has people that are experts in your area. He wants to get those people across your path. When you meet with these mentors, value their time and acknowledge their expertise with ultimate respect.

PROVERBS 12:15

The way of a fool is right in his own eyes: but he that
hearkeneth unto counsel is wise.

JUST LOOKING OR LUSTING

Be aware of your flesh when it begins to rise.
The flesh is the part of you that's always willing to compromise.
The flesh wants to take the path of least resistance.
As you walk in the spirit, it will become more and more persistent.

Gary had a problem of lusting after beautiful women. He desired to be free from this sin. But Gary would look and look every time he saw a beautiful woman. His mind would begin to lust after these women, and if the women would glance back at him, he would think to himself, "They want to holler at me!" Then Gary would pursue them, by asking them for their telephone number – just to become friends, of course. As the telephone conversations increased, Gary would propose a cordial visit. During this visiting phase is when Gary would find himself unable to avoid the temptation that followed. God explained to him how to get delivered from this sin. The next time a beautiful woman comes across his path, he should form the habit of looking just one time. Don't swivel his head over and over to look at the woman. Stop it at its onslaught! Or stop it in the beginning phase before it gets out of hand. Once it gets moving, it's a lot harder to stop it. It is a lot easier to stop it when it's standing still.

Stay away from the fire so you don't get burned. Your flesh will always try to get its way. It will try to convince you to get close to the fire, and that the fire is really not that hot. But once you're close enough, you will get burned. Your flesh will always take you farther than you should go. Build your spirit man and your flesh will get weaker. Your spirit should always lead in whatever you do!

PROVERBS 13:14

The law of the wise is a fountain of life, to
depart from the snares of death.

PROVERBS 14:2

He that walketh in his uprightness feareth the LORD:
but he that is perverse in his ways despiseth him.

PROVERBS 14:12

There is a way which seemeth right unto a man, but the
end thereof are the ways of death.

IT'S BETTER TO GIVE THAN TO RECEIVE

Giving is always better than receiving.
Don't wait to see, just began believing.
When needs seem to grow.
Find a need and begin to sow!

Michael is a giver. One Friday, I gave him a five dollar bill. That Sunday while in a church service, the offering plate was making its way around. When it got to Michael, he put his five dollar bill in the offering plate without hesitation – it was all the money he had. His parents didn't tell Michael to give an offering.

Shortly after giving the offering, a woman gave him a ten dollar bill. He received a fast return on the seed he had sown! Michael has learned a valuable lesson at a very early age. He gave without hesitation and without fear of not having. He had the faith not to worry about where more money would come from; he just gave what he had at the time of need. Whenever his parents or anyone else asked for anything, he was always willing to give.

Give! Give! Give of your money, of your time, of your possessions! Give! Never allow possessions to grab a hold of your heart. God gives to us to get it through us. It's not intended to stop with you! Holding on is how this world's system operates, but God's system says give and that's how you will receive. God's team is undefeated and will continue this winning streak always. Roll with God's team!

PROVERBS 11:24

There is that scattereth, and yet increaseth;
and there is that withholdeth more than is meet,
but is tendeth to poverty.

SQUASH IT QUICKLY

Pride is the Devil's baby.
He sends thoughts to sway you from doing well to
considering doing bad as a maybe.
Stay humble and the voice of God will speak.
Avoid being a know it all; take the path of the meek.

There were two brothers, Aaron and Mason. One day, the two were involved in a heated argument. It wasn't anything serious, but both refused to back down. Both had formed the mindset that they would hurt each other before backing down. In an instance, Aaron's heart changed. Extending his hand, he said, "My fault. I'm sorry, bro!" Then he hugged his brother. The strife between the two was eradicated in an instant. The beef they had was suddenly squashed due to Aaron hugging his brother. This humbling act on Aaron's behalf slammed the door to the Devil! Mason suddenly wasn't angry anymore either. It was difficult for him to continue in a rage once Aaron had decided to squash the whole matter.

Pride is something we all battle. This is what got Satan kicked out of Heaven, so he will definitely use it to make us stumble. Recognize when pride is on the horizon. Humble yourself. The world believes in comments seated in pride like, "Don't let them get away with that!" Or "I won't back down!" or "I will get them back!" or "I won't let it go!" All of these mindsets will keep us operating in pride and allow the Devil the opportunity to destroy us. Let's close the door to the Devil by repenting and humbling ourselves quickly!

PROVERBS 16:18

Pride goeth before destruction and a
haughty spirit before a fall.

GOD SPEAKS THROUGH HIS WORD

Make the Word of God your most coveted treasure.
Tons of money can't compare, it can't measure.
It will set your life on its proper course.
Guide your decisions, leaving behind a path of no remorse.

One day while looking out of the window of his house, Andre saw a prostitute with a man inside a car parked on the side of his home. On another day, Andre was looking out of the same window, and saw a known drug dealer from the neighborhood exchange a zip lock baggie of drugs for money with another man. Andre thought to himself, "I need to move from here!" But his wife was pregnant. They had two car notes and a mortgage. Because a better neighborhood would mean a higher mortgage payment, it seemed impossible.

While reading God's Word, God spoke these words to Andre: "Move. If you want to move, then move!" By faith, Andre said, "Ok, Lord, I'm going to do it!" Andre, his pregnant wife, and all their debt began the process of selling their home and finding a new home. After the process was completed, God had gone far above what they had expected. Someone paid $95,000 cash, the exact price they were asking for their home. Not only were they able to pay off their home, but they had $11,000 left after the closing to put down on their new home, which helped decrease the loan amount. The new neighborhood was much more peaceful and they never had a problem paying the new mortgage!

For any problem, question, or anything in life, the Word of God has the solution! For any marriage situation, parenting situation, career path selection, spouse selection, God's Word is your source. Search the scriptures as if you are searching for a hidden treasure.

PROVERBS 30:5

Every word of God is pure: he is a shield unto them that put their trust in him.

SHOWER YOUR MOTHER

Your mother is your Queen.
Always express kind words and gestures to lift her self-esteem.
Acknowledge her on all special days.
Show her love in many different ways.

This is a story of a Proverbs 31 woman. Fredricka was told by doctors that becoming pregnant and having a baby could be life threatening. But by the grace of God, she became pregnant. By faith, she carried her son, before her blood pressure increased to a dangerously high level. She was rushed to the hospital and told she would have to deliver the baby prematurely, and by C Section. Her baby boy arrived early, but was healthy. And after the doctor closed her abdomen, Mom began recovering well. A tremendous sacrifice was made to bring her son into this world. She now works as a wife, mother, and employee -- just to name a few titles. She works tirelessly cleaning her home from top to bottom. Not surface cleaning, but intricate detailed cleaning. She does laundry and irons all the clothes for the family on the weekend for the following week. And has, while working a full time job, sold crystal, Mary Kay, and managed a vending machine. She cooks meals for her family and is respected and loved by her husband and children. She prays for and visits the families of her friends and co-workers who are hospitalized.

Your mother will always be there for you. I believe God created her heart to be so forgiving toward her children, that no matter what they do, she will be there for them always. Love, protect, and respect your mother for the length of your days on this earth. Serve her always!

PROVERBS 4:3

For I was my father's son, tender and only
beloved in the sight of my mother.

WORDS MATTER

It's not always good to speak your mind.
Preview the words beforehand on the screen of your mind.
Beware of the damage words can cause.
Before speaking take a brief pause.

One summer afternoon, best friends Mitch and George were preparing for a double date. George was dating Tracy and she suggested that Mitch should come along and meet her best friend Trina. When the four of them got together, Mitch and Trina were instantly attracted physically to each other. Mitch thought Trina was beautiful. She enjoyed basketball, so they talked and laughed for hours. They walked in the park after a fabulous dinner. The four drove home at the end of their date, Mitch and Trina sat in the back seat playfully engaging each other. Mitch then said playfully, "You are acting just like your father!"

Trina went off on Mitch. She cursed him with words so harsh, the words seemed to be coming from the pit of hell. Mitch had forgotten about an earlier conversation they had in which Trina revealed her disdain for her father. Mitch apologized with deep sympathy, but Trina refused to receive his apology and continued to curse him. When the car stopped, Trina jumped out and slammed the door. Mitch never saw or spoke with Trina again. Those few words that Mitch had spoken cost him a friendship. As small as those words were to Mitch, they were straight from hell in the mind of Trina.

The power of life and death are found in what we speak. Words spoken from our mouths can be compared to bullets fired from a gun. Once a bullet is fired from a gun, there is no way it can be retracted. The same is true of words. Once they leave our mouths, there is no way they can be re-tracked. Speak words that uplift; don't speak words that tear down. Direct the words you speak with a positive purpose. Use your words like bricks to build your future one by one!

PROVERBS 21:23

Whoso keepeth his mouth and his tongue keepeth his soul from troubles.

NEVER GIVE UP

When times get tough, remember it's only temporary.
While the storm is raging, the storm is so scary.
Press on until you make it to the other side.
If you stop in the midst of the storm,
you are sure to remain inside.

Preston was attempting to live right for the Lord. No sex until marriage was his game plan. He was introduced to a woman who had two children. Ignoring all the signs that this relationship may not be from God, Preston dove head first into the relationship. Preston wanted to please God more than anything, so instead of living in lust, he asked the woman to marry him. He thought he was doing the right thing, but was really blinded by lust. After trying to take care of two children from two different fathers, and a wife whose mindset came from one of the worst neighborhoods in the city, his wife filed for a divorce by certified mail. During the divorce proceedings, Preston was given the house they had bought together, but he was ordered to refinance it and give his ex-wife all the equity, which was about $7,000. His ex-wife also was given all the furniture in the house that was worth anything. Heartbroken and distressed, Preston plummeted into a deep depression. He really couldn't afford the house because the mortgage note had increased since the refinance. Although struggling, he paid the mortgage and all his other bills. To cut down on cost, he would unplug all his appliances and turn off his heat while he was at work. It seemed Preston was down for the count. But after some time, he prayed for a Proverbs 31 woman, and eventually, God answered his prayer and brought him the wife of his dreams!

Life will knock you down more times than you can count. Never stay down! Always get b up quickly! The only way to fail is to stay down. I don't care what curve balls life throws be willing to swing at the next pitch. Keep following God until the end of this race. He always get you back on course. The only way He stops guiding is when you stay down

---

PROVERBS 24:16

For a just man falleth seven times, and riseth up ag
but the wicked shall fall into mischief.

GET WISDOM FIRST

Seek wisdom before you make a move.
Wisdom was there with God in the beginning,
when He made major moves.
Seeking wisdom should always come in number
one in the ranks.
Wisdom is more valuable than a combination
of all the banks.

There was a group of men, all armed with dull axes. They all headed into a forest full of large trees, except one man named Terrance. Although apprehensive, Terrance remained behind to sharpen his ax. As he continued to sharpen his ax, he watched all the other men begin chopping the trees. But very little progress was being made on the trees, due to their dull blades. Once Terrance had sharpened his blade razor sharp, he headed for a specific tree, chopped in a specific spot on the tree, and his tree fell to the ground.

Terrance's sharpening the ax was a symbol of seeking wisdom first. It seemed as if the other guys were getting ahead because they got out of the gate quickly. But because their blades were dull, the whole process was flawed. Without seeking wisdom first, we will all be engaged in wrong careers and relationships.

Always seek wisdom first. Don't be hurried into any endeavor. Understand the consequences of a choice before the decision is made. Pour your heart into seeking wisdom and then rest. The path you seek will be cleared by wisdom and your steps are now free from obstruction.

PROVERBS 4:7

Wisdom is the principal thing: therefore get wisdom:
and with all thy getting get understanding.

RESPECT YOUR ELDERS

You are the future, but your elders are your link to the past.
Disrespecting them is a way to decline extremely fast.
Maintain respect no matter how their lifestyle may appear.
Humble yourself, even if you've taken off in your career.

When Myles was a young boy, he witnessed several events that changed the respect he had toward his father. First, while he was seated in the back seat of their car, Myles pleaded with his father to stop choking his mother as she was gasping for air. The second incident was when his dad had a girlfriend he would spend all his time with. He would hide the girlfriend in the back seat of his car, and ask young Myles not to tell his mom about the girlfriend. The third incident was once young Myles was with his dad and they went through an alley, climbed up a back outside staircase and through a door. Once inside, they met with a man who gave his dad a needle and a small hose. His dad wrapped his arm with the small hose and shot himself with the needle in his arm.

As Myles grew older, he became bitter toward his dad for not being there for him. But God touched his heart and after a lengthy conversation, he forgave his dad. Their relationship grew until his dad eventually passed away. Although his dad wasn't there while he was growing up, Miles had respect for his dad in his later years.

No matter how bad a parent one might think they've had, God said to respect them and you'll have a long life. Take care of your elders as they grow old. Even when you become successful, remain humble in the presence of your elders.

PROVERBS 23:22

Hearken unto thy father that begat thee,
and despise not thy mother when she is old.

AN ATTITUDE OF HUMILITY IS ALWAYS BETTER

A humble request is always better than a selfish demand.
People respond more favorably when please is attached to an
outstretched hand.
After a request is granted, always have a sense of gratitude.
Even if the request is rejected, never leave with a bad attitude.

Daniel and the three Hebrew boys were slaves under the dictatorship of King Nebuchadnezzar. Daniel, a child of the Most High God and a devout follower of God's Word, promised God that he wouldn't defile himself by eating the King's meat. But Daniel had one problem: the King had declared that Daniel along with all the other slaves would be fed the King's meat and wine for three years and after the three years, they would stand before the King. Now imagine what would happen if a slave were to tell a King he wasn't going to obey a command he had given. God had given Daniel favor with one of the King's princes. Listen to the tone Daniel used in speaking with the prince about not eating the King's meat. He requested of the prince that he not defile himself. Now the prince feared disobeying the King would endanger his head. But Daniel said, "I beseech thee, ten days; and let them give us pulse to eat, and water to drink." The word beseech that Daniel used is sort of like saying I beg you. Because of the humility in Daniel's tone, the King agreed to what he proposed. And after the ten days, Daniel appeared fairer and fatter in flesh than the children that ate the King's meat.

Respect is huge in dealing with people. Please and thank you are words that convey respect, kindness, and gratitude. Your attitude will sometimes determine how others will treat you. You control your attitude, no matter what has happened to you in your past. Keep the right attitude! Remember: How something is said is sometimes more important than what is said.

PROVERBS 6:12

A naughty person, a wicked man, walketh
with a froward mouth.

ALL ABOARD

Wrath was headed to all mankind; Jesus shed His Blood
and the wrath for believers came to a pause.
To get unbelievers saved has become the number one cause.
Help God keep your brothers and sisters from the pit of hell.
The promises of God are the products you'll sell.

Detective Johnson, a fierce investigator, had the opportunity to talk with hundreds of individuals who had committed various kinds of crimes. He saw his career as monotonous and without purpose. He began to feel down about what he did every day at work. He saw some of the same individuals, committing the same crimes, and that became discouraging. One day, God spoke to him and instructed him to start ministering to the individuals he came in contact with on his job. God wanted him to view each interview he had as an opportunity to win another soul. Detective Johnson had a renewed fervor for his job.

He began to pray before he entered the interview room. And God's Spirit would show up and touch the hearts of the individuals he talked with. Detective Johnson prays for the individuals he interviews. He speaks the scriptures and words that God leads him to say, and at times, he is the only Jesus the people will ever see. Inside the interview rooms, Detective Johnson has witnessed countless miracles on account of that he has begun to invite God into the room. His partnership with God has resulted in hundreds of souls being saved.

God said it is wise to win souls. Use all the talents and gifts that God has put inside of you to win people to the Lord. The return of our Lord Jesus is ever closer, so every day the focus should be to win more people before He returns. Before the Lord returns, use what God has put inside of you to get all aboard, before the rapture occurs.

PROVERBS 11:30

The fruit of the righteous is a tree of life;
and he that winneth souls is wise.

GEAR MATTERS

When headed to a place of importance,
put time into what you wear.
Don't fall into the trap of thinking it doesn't
matter what you wear.
Whatever the occasion, aim to look presentable.
Appearance will help you come across more reputable.

Todd was attempting to reform his life from a former street hustler. He had never worked a job, just earned quick cash from his many street hustles. Todd's gear consisted of long white T-Shirts, sagging pants, and white gym shoes. His hair was wild and his beard was umkept. Some of the words Todd commonly mispronounced were "Dem" instead of "Them," "Da" instead of "The," "Dose" instead of "Those." Todd had taken all of these habits into the many interviews he had previously gone to. Not once was he contacted or called in for an interview. Todd was informed of the changes he needed to make in his appearance and his speech. Todd began wearing a navy suit with a dress shirt and a tie. The dress shoes he wore were polished. His hair was cut neatly and his mustache was trimmed. Todd then focused on pronouncing each word he spoke more thoroughly. Shortly after making these slight adjustments, Todd was hired for a job!

Your appearance does matter. It represents who you are. Before any words come out of your mouth, your appearance will speak volumes. It may be wrong for people to judge you based on your appearance, but they will. And they will judge you based on your speaking ability. Remember, you only get one chance to make a first impression! When you are out with your friends, certain gear and conversation is acceptable; just learn what's appropriate at what time.

PROVERBS 9:6

Forsake the foolish, and live; and go in the
way of understanding.

JUST BUZZING

Addictions are formed over a period of time;
they don't start out that way.
The process begins and then day by day,
a sip here and a sip there.
Soon, you wake up one morning wondering how you arrived.

Abusing alcohol or drugs is an escape route. It is used by some who have hit a wall in life they perceive as unbreakable. Some start out drinking socially. They drink when they're out with friends and before long, they're hooked.

One night, I went out with friends. We drank malt liquor beer to get a buzz faster. We didn't know the malt liquor they put inside the beer was poison. That's why we got a buzz faster.

After drinking the beer, we all drove separately and met at a house party. At the party, they served different wines and liquor; I consumed some of them all. As I danced with this female – a complete stranger – she asked if I wanted to go to her place and get higher. Buzzing, the room spinning, I thought I'd better make it upstairs to the bathroom. I made it to the bathroom, and it felt like I was vomiting up all my organs! Then I found myself driving home in my mother's car, crossing over the double yellow line in the road. By the grace of God, I made it home!

Do not put yourself in a situation where you have no control of yourself. Stay clear from using alcohol and drugs. Using just one time could take you on a long journey of abuse. Sometimes many years are wasted chasing addictions.

The alcohol and drugs could be laced with other addictive properties. These drugs alter the mind and destroy the body, which is the temple where God dwells.
Keep the temple Holy!

PROVERBS 20:1
Wine is a mocker, strong drink is ragging;
and whosoever is deceived thereby is not wise.

LEAD AS THE MAN SHOULD

To lead first receive proper instructions.
The Father is the source; where all successful
paths generate there flow.
Sit at the Master's feet, like a sponge soak
in all the wisdom He has in order to lead.
So that those that follow you are fed the proper substance.

It's almost time for bed, but there's one dreaded task that must be completed first. Dante is ten years old. Although ten years old may seem young for this daunting task, his mom and sister are afraid of completing the task. So Dante has to become the man of his household. He grabs a bucket, fills it with water and a cleaning solution, dips the trap inside the solution, scrubs it with a small toothbrush, and dries it with a dry towel. Dante then retrieves the huge block of welfare cheese from the refrigerator. He slices a small piece of cheese from the block. He also snaps a small piece of thread from his mother's spool. He places the slice of cheese on the small metal plate, and then wraps the thread around the cheese. Dante places the trap underneath the kitchen sink, next to the large hole in the floor board used as a doorway from the crawl space, which was created by the constant gnawing. Dante is now ready for bed. He climbs up the small ladder that separates his bed, which sits on top of his sister's bed.

During the night as Dante slept, he is awakened by the gnawing and screeching within the walls. The noise sounds like someone sliding their nails down a chalk board. This noise is interrupted only by Dante pounding his fist on the wall.

The next morning, Dante was awakened by the clock's blaring alarm! It's time to get ready for school, but first Dante has to complete the daunting task. Dante opens the cabinet door underneath the kitchen sink. One side of the trap was snapped onto the neck of a plump brown rat. Dante hesitantly grabbed the metal bar that was slammed down on the rat's neck, ever so cautiously, so not to touch the splattered blood. He then slides the rat into a brown paper bag, takes it out back to the alley and dumps the bag into a brown dumpster. This task would be done by Dante everyday for as long as he could remember. His father's absence lead to this task and many other tasks Dante unwillingly completed.

Teach me to do thy will; for thou art my God:
thy spirit is good; lead me into the land of uprightness.

Give instruction to a wise man, and he will be yet wiser:
teach a just man, and he will increase in learning.

DON'T PUT IT OFF

Taking care of business quickly is a good habit to form.
This can keep you from getting caught in future storms.
Opportunities come to those who are diligent.
Procrastinating will cost you blessings that are Heaven sent.

Melvin was in ninth grade, just starting out at a high school. He didn't know any of the other students except his cousin. So Melvin began to skip school with his cousin, and play video games at a nearby store. Melvin's grades plummeted as his absences increased. More than anything, Melvin wanted to play on the basketball team at his new school, but he had lost his focus because of his new environment. He continued to put off going to his classes because he was the new kid in every class. Melvin did just enough of his school work to get by. He tried out for the basketball team and made the cut. He was a new member on the basketball team, and he began to meet all kinds of new friends. As the end of the report card marking drew near, Melvin's English teacher gave out progress reports. Melvin had a 1.83 grade point average. His coach suspended him from the basketball team immediately. The coach explained to Melvin that each player on the team had to maintain a 2.0 grade point average. Melvin was devastated by this news!

Because this was just a progress report, Melvin went to his English teacher and begged her to change his F to a D-, in order to raise his grade point average from a 1.83 to a 2.0. His teacher told him that she had never done anything like that, but she was going to do it this time. She emphatically explained to Melvin that if he didn't begin to come to class regularly and turn in assignments, he would fail her class on the next report card marking. Melvin stopped procrastinating and began completing his assignments and went on to raise his grade in her class, and rejoin the basketball team!

In whatever you do, do it with excellence. Get there early! Stay late! Don't put off until tomorrow what you can do today. Diligence will cause the world to take notice and bring you in favor with important people. When business is at hand, complete it without hesitation. Putting things off just creates more stress, unnecessary stress!

PROVERBS 22:29

Seest thou a man diligent in his business? He shall
stand before kings; he shall not stand before mean men.

HURDLES ARE MEANT TO BE JUMPED/GOD KNOWS

Road blocks are in place as you approach them don't stop.
Keep moving when you get close jump over the top.
Only if you stop will this race of life come to an end.
Back up to your feet quickly soldier! Make this your life's trend.

William felt God was calling him into the ministry. But his job schedule didn't favor the move to enroll in the school of ministry that God was urging him to make. The school hours were 8am-12pm, Monday through Friday. His work schedule was 11am-7pm, and his off days varied. William attempted to persuade God that the supervisors at work weren't Christians, and that they wouldn't allow him to go to school during those hours. There weren't any other positions at his job that he could switch to, that would afford him the opportunity to go to the school of ministry. But God would not listen to William and his reasons why it wouldn't work. God continued to press upon William's heart, which led him in the direction of registering for his classes at the school of ministry. Still unsure of how this would work out, William just believed that God would take care of everything. God told him what supervisor to approach. William approached his supervisor and told him that he had registered in classes at the school of ministry from the hours of 8am-12pm, Monday through Friday. His supervisor angrily responded, "Who told you to do this?" William stated, "God told me to do it!" William attended the school of ministry for two years and completed the program. His supervisor allowed him to work 12:30pm-8:30pm Monday through Friday.

God knows where we are supposed to be. As we acknowledge Him, He said He will direct our paths. Before we make any moves, we should acknowledge Him and He will tell us which way we should go. And as we consistently pack His Word in our hearts, we will hear His voice more clearly. Stepping out in faith is how we are going to be able to take God's Word from just words to being manifested in our lives. When He reveals something to us, we must act on what He has told us. It doesn't matter how the circumstances may look; we have to just believe God and move as He leads us.

PROVERBS 20:24

Man's goings are of the Lord; how can a man
then understand his own way?

STAY STRONG

A life may stand in the balance, in need of your assistance.
Your strength will prove valuable when life brings resistance.
When called upon, let your strength rise as a hero.
The strength you possess depends upon the workouts you sow.

Marty played point guard for a division two University. One day during practice, his coach said, "Marty, go beyond the point in which you think you can't go any farther!" Marty didn't understand what his coach was saying at the time. But later, he would get a revelation of what his coach meant. During spring recruiting, their team welcomed a player named Allen from a division one University. Allen had to sit out and not play for a year because of the transfer, but he could work out with the team. Marty and Allen were paired up together for their workouts. One day during practice, their coach put one minute on the scoreboard and told the team to run 17 sprints within the minute. If anyone didn't make it, they would immediately line it up and run 17 sprints again. And if everyone still didn't make it, they would immediately line it up and run 9 sprints in thirty seconds. Normally, Marty wouldn't go all out because one of his teammates that was 6'9, 300lbs. would never make the time.

But Marty felt he had to compete because he was paired with Allen. Allen ran every single sprint as hard as he could. Marty was forced to do the same. After all the sprints were completed, Marty felt as if he was going to die, but he didn't. Marty now saw what it felt like to go beyond the point in which he thought he couldn't go. It was sort of a breakthrough for him. Now, every drill he did was done in this fashion, and his game began to improve drastically!

Discipline yourself to go beyond your comfort level. This is where improvement lies! Control yourself and you won't have to be controlled by others. Restrain yourself and you won't have to be restrained by others. Exercising helps discipline the body. It helps develop the habit of pushing the body when it doesn't want to be pushed. Exercise helps keep the body and mind strong and prepared for the trials of life.

PROVERBS 25:28

He that hath no rule over his own spirit is like
a city that is broken down, and without walls.

STAY THE COURSE

In life, one wrong turn can turn into a prolonged detour.
Darkness can dim the path of those once projected to soar.
The path God has for you is obstruction free,
So you can focus on who Gods wants you to be.

One night, Deshawn and a group of his friends were walking down a busy road within their neighborhood. The street was well lit by the street lights and the headlights of the cars that passed by. They decided to take a shortcut – a turn down a dark alley. As they cut through the alley, a guy turned down the alley on a bicycle. Deshawn and his friends heard the strangest sound. It sounded like something being detached from Velcro. But as they looked with their mouths open wide, the guy on the bike was ripping a sawed off shotgun from the crossbar on the bicycle. The shot gun was heavily taped on the crossbar of the bike. The gunman then yelled, "Where is my dog?" As Deshawn began backing away from his friends toward the rear of the alley, the gunman walked toward Deshawn, hands shaking, pointing the shotgun at his chest. Deshawn thought to himself, "Should I run and possibly get shot in the back? Or should I stand here and get shot in the chest?" Deshawn's friends screamed for him to keep his hands up! The gunman, now standing directly in front of Deshawn with the shotgun, opened Deshawn's white jacket. The gunman then said, "You lucky this jacket ain't black or you a be dead!" The gunman got on his bike and rode off. Deshawn found out that a group of guys had taken the gunman's puppy Rottweiler. Deshawn and his friends immediately returned to the well lit street and continued their journey.

Stay on the path that God has for you. Your protection and all other blessings lie on this path. No other path is better! People will attempt to get you off this path for all of your days. God's path has all the light to see everything you need.

PROVERBS 4:26 (AMPLIFIED)

Consider well the path of your feet, and let all your
ways be established and ordered aright.

YOU CAN ALWAYS ASK THE FATHER

Always feel free to approach the Father.
When you've done wrong is not the time to
head for an island.
God is aware that you're going to do wrong while
it's still only a thought.
Not asking the Father, only means you can't
expect an answer from Him.

Mack was a blessed man of God. One of the many blessings he possessed was a company car. His company provided the fuel and maintenance for the car as well. One day, he locked some of his personal items inside the glove box. He unlocked the glove box, but it wouldn't open. He eventually had to break the entire lock and pry the glove box open with a screwdriver to get his things out. He had completely destroyed the glove box. A couple days later while still trying to figure out how he would get the glove box repaired, Mack was driving his car, while extremely sleepy. He was stopped at a red light and fell asleep. As he woke to his car rolling forward, he was startled. He jammed on what he thought was the brake, but he found that it was the gas pedal. He slammed into the car in front of him, and that car slammed into the car in front of it.

No sooner than when the damage from these prior two incidents were repaired, Mack was driving the car up an exit ramp. He hit the brake, the car continued to slide, slamming into the rear of a car that was stopped in front of him. He thought to himself, "This can't be happening!" Although he had asked God to help him in the two prior incidents, Mack still asked the Father for help in this current situation. The Father heard his prayer and helped him in this situation.

Whenever you find yourself in a jam, whether it was your own fault or someone else's, go to the Father. He knows what you have done anyhow. He is waiting for you to come to Him and ask for help. To ask for help is to walk in humility and God gives grace to the humble. He is not just God; He is the Father! The Father understands His children; He is not just the judge with a gavel looking to slam it down with a scream of guilty, every time we make a mistake. He is the loving Father who extends mercy and grace to His children, even when they've done wrong.

Every word of God is pure: he is a shield unto them
that put their trust in him.

WATCH YOUR COMPANY

Bad company corrupts good character.
Watch the people you keep company
with like a detailed inspector.
When you're constantly around them,
subtle changes in your character will occur.
Sometimes you have to make a switch in the friends you prefer.

Listen to this story in the 1st chapter of Proverbs verses 10 through 19 (The Message), on why you should avoid sinners when they try to entice you.

"Dear friend, if bad companions tempt you; don't go along with them.
If they say-"Let's go out and raise some hell. Let's beat up some old man, mug some old woman. Let's pick them clean and get them ready for their funerals. We'll load up on top-quality loot. We'll haul it home by the truckload. Join us for the time of your life! With us, it's share and share alike!"- Oh, friend, don't give them a second look; don't listen to them for a minute. They're racing to a very bad end, hurrying to ruin everything they lay hands on. Nobody robs a bank with everyone watching, yet that's what these people are doing- they're doing themselves in. When you grab all you can get, that's what happens: the more you get, the less you are."

There are people in the world that will bring you down if you associate with them. They may be people whom you consider to be your friends. But if anyone suggests that you do anything against the Word of God, they aren't really your friends. Real friends will discourage you from doing anything wrong. The decisions you make early will follow you into your adult years. Don't allow peer pressure to influence you into doing something that might haunt you later on in life. Walk away from these people. Even if they call you weak, or scary, or a punk, don't be moved by the comments they make. And know that if you decide to harm innocent people, the harm you do to them is really being done to yourself.

PROVERBS 1:15
My son walk not thou in the way with them,
refrain thy foot from their path:

DON'T BE SEDUCED BY HER BEAUTY

Some females are looking for an unsuspecting catch.
If you're entranced by their beauty,
your heart they'll seek to snatch.
Outer beauty is deceptive when inner
beauty doesn't match.
Tightly close your eyes, for your desire
of her beauty can lead to your demise.

Listen to this story in the 7th chapter of Proverbs verses 6 through 27 (The Message), which details an account of a young man being seduced by a beautiful woman.

"As I stood at the window of my house looking out through the shutters, watching the mindless crowd stroll by, I spotted a young man without any sense arriving at the corner of the street where she lived, and then turning up the path to her house. It was dusk, the evening coming on, the darkness thickening into night. Just then, a woman met him-she'd been lying in wait for him, dressed to seduce him. Brazen and brash she was, restless and roaming, never at home, walking the streets, loitering in the mall, hanging out at every corner in town.

"She threw her arms around him and kissed him, boldly took his arm and said, 'I've got all the makings for a feast-today I made offerings, my vows are all paid, so now I've come to find you, hoping to catch sight of your face-and here you are! I've spread fresh, clean sheets on my bed, colorful imported linens. My bed is aromatic with spices and exotic fragrances. Come, let's make love all night, spend the night in ecstatic lovemaking! My husband's not home; he's away on business, and he won't be back for a month.' Soon she has him eating out of her hand, bewitched by her honeyed speech. Before you know it, he's trotting behind her, like a calf led to the butcher shop. Like a stag lured into ambush and then shot with an arrow. Like a bird flying into a net not knowing that it's flying life is over. So, friends, listen to me, take these words of mine most seriously. Don't fool around with a woman like that; don't even stroll through her neighborhood. Countless victims come under her spell; she's the death of many a poor man. She runs a halfway house to hell, fits you out with a shroud and a coffin."

Lust not after her beauty in thine heart, neither let her take thee with her eyelids.

LAZY FREE ZONE

God has said to look at the ant be wise.
They are extremely diligent despite their size.
Without a boss they work very hard.
The wisdom within this insect should be
held at the highest regard.

Listen to the Gill's Exposition of the Entire Bible, which summarizes the 6th chapter of Proverbs verses 6 through 8.

"Consider her ways; what diligence and industry it uses in providing food; which, though a small, weak, feeble creature, yet will travel over flints and stones, climb trees, enter into towers, barns, cellars, places high and low, in search of food, never hinder, but help one another in carrying their burdens; prepare little cells to put their provisions in, and are so built as to secure them from rain; and if at any time their corn is wet, they bring out and dry it, and bite off the ends of it, that it may not grow."

The basketball great Allen Iverson, at 6'0 tall and 160lbs, shows how his diligence, despite his size, led to greatness. In his junior year in high school, he led his team to the state championship in football. When interviewed after the victory, he was asked how he felt about the championship victory. He said, "Now we'll go win it in basketball, too!" And a couple of months later when his basketball season had ended, he had led his basketball team to a state championship, also. He won a state championship in football and basketball within the same season. He also was named player of the year in football and basketball in the state of Virginia during his junior year!

Stay busy always! Create a habit of doing what you don't necessarily feel like doing. As a matter of fact, purpose in your heart to do things you don't desire to do because it appears difficult to complete. Don't get into the habit of trying to get out of difficult tasks. Overcome your difficulties!

PROVERBS 6:6

Go to the ant, thou sluggard, consider
her ways, and be wise.

FAITHFULNESS IN THE TIME OF TROUBLE

If you are faithful with another's, then
God will give you your own.
God sends people on your path to teach you,
before you branch out on your own.
God can always be trusted, even in the time of trouble.
Like a full set of teeth and two strong feet,
God has your back on the double.

Kevin was walking home from the store one day. His friend Eddie saw him and approached him with a proposition. He said, "Come play basketball with me at the park?" Now Kevin knew that this park Eddie was referring to was known for trouble in the neighborhood. Kevin said no at first, but Eddie pleaded with Kevin to come and play basketball with him. Kevin wanted badly to play basketball, but didn't want any trouble. Kevin decided to accept Eddie's offer to play at the park. As they walked into the park, a guy named Ardell, from Kevin's school, walked up to him and started shadow boxing toward his face. Kevin heard another older guy from the neighborhood named Damon yell out, "Hit that nigga in his jaw, Ardell!" Ardell then grabbed Kevin by his collar. Kevin immediately knocked Ardell's hands down. Kevin knowing how things went down in his neighborhood, knew he was going to have to fight Ardell. The only problem is Ardell's brother and friends are all at the park, and his friend Eddie is nowhere to be found. As Kevin and Ardell begin to fight, Kevin is starting to get the best of Ardell, and Kevin gets a glimpse of Ardell's brother and his friends running over to help him. They all tried to jump Kevin, but he broke away and ran away from the park. Kevin never saw his friend Eddie during any of this, much less did he receive any help from him that day. Eddie was an unfaithful friend!

God's faithful to us! If He makes a promise in His Word, He is faithful to keep it! We must also be faithful. If we promise to do something, we must keep our word. Even when trouble arises, we must stick to our guns. The Word is true, whether we're in a peaceful environment or in the midst of a fight. If you are with a friend and trouble arises, never run out on your friend. Help him! As we prove ourselves faithful, God will promote us. A big part in becoming a leader is learning to be faithful. God can become confident in us as we become faithful.

Confidence in an unfaithful man in time of trouble is like a broken tooth, and a foot out of joint.

KEEP LACK iN THE REARVIEW

When life gets tough and you seek motivation,
View successful people during their preparation.
Sometimes the rearview mirror has poverty
staring in their face.
Think on what will keep you in the winner's place.

Every year during the start of conditioning, Corey's basketball team had to run a timed mile. Corey played point guard, and the point guards were grouped together, and were required to run the fastest time. Next were the swing men, which consisted of shooting guards and small forwards. And last were the big men, which consisted of power forwards and centers. Usually, the team ran the mile on their track. Running four times around the track equaled one mile, so the guys could pace themselves. But this year, their coach had marked off a straight path on a nature trail that equaled one mile. As the team began to run, Corey and another teammate were running side by side, neither one of them gave an inch. Corey began to feel as if he couldn't go any further nor keep his current pace. Corey began to think of some rough times he encountered during his childhood. He remembered one time as a young child, in the midst of a very cold winter, his family was unable to pay the heat bill and their heat was turned off. He remembered lying in his bed, fully covered by a large blanket, balled into a fetal position, and still feeling extremely cold. This thought inspired Corey to run past his competition – to run faster and faster until he crossed the finish line in first place. Although he was extremely tired, this thought gave him an added boast of energy.

Stay hungry! Stay motivated! Never become complacent! Strive to do your best continuously. Grow where you are. Sometimes in life, you may have the tendency to get down. Find the motivation to get up quickly and get back into the race of life. When you work hard at your craft, you will be successful. Hard work does pay off.

PROVERBS 24:30-34 (THE MESSAGE)

One day I walked by the field of an old lazybones,
and then passed the vineyard of a lout; They were
overgrown with weeds, thick with thistles, all the

fences broken down. I took a long look and pondered what I saw; the fields preached me a sermon and I listened: A nap here, a nap there, a day off here, a day off there, sit back, take it easy-do you know what comes next? Just this: You can look forward to a dirt-poor life, with poverty as your permanent houseguest!

PREPARATION PAVES THE WAY TO OPPORTUNITY

When preparation meets opportunity is
when success is hatched.
Stay ready and competition will be no match.
As you live, be ready, for change is evident.
When blessings rain down, you'll know they're Heaven sent.

Marvin was beginning his junior year in high school and played on their basketball team. He had played on the junior varsity basketball team the previous year. This season the team was full of seniors, which decreased Marvin's chance of seeing significant playing time. Marvin controlled the factors that he could control. He drastically increased his grade point average and worked extremely hard to improve his basketball skills. Marvin worked hard in practice, but never received any playing time in the games.

One day, Marvin came to practice as normal, and his coach approached him with good news. His coach said one of his teammates, a starter, didn't receive a 2.0 grade point average and wouldn't be able to remain on the team. The coach said they planned on moving Marvin into the vacant position his teammate left. The next game arrived and Marvin was placed into the starting line-up. He was extremely nervous. Marvin started the game and played awesome. His team won and Marvin scored a team high 14 points. The local newspaper's article on the game highlighted Marvin's performance.

Prepare yourself diligently in your craft! When opportunity arises, there is no time to get ready. Some opportunities will never surface again, so you may only get one shot. Take advantage of all the opportunities that come your way. When you prepare, God is placed in a position to bring the victory!

PROVERBS 21:31 (THE MESSAGE)
Do your best, prepare for the worst-then
trust God to bring victory.

GOD'S WISDOM BRINGS GOD'S RESULTS

Sometimes what others are doing may appear to be cool.
Find out what God says is the rule.
Following everyone else can cause you to lose out.
Heed God's voice, and then move with no doubt.

Kevin had just turned 15 years old — the magic number in which he could obtain employment. He completed application after application, waiting for a response. No one called, so he began to feel that maybe he wouldn't be able to find a job. One day, he filled out an application at a local fast food restaurant. A week had gone by and he still hadn't heard anything. While sitting at home, God spoke to him. God told Kevin to find out who was in charge of hiring and give them a call. Kevin called the next morning and found that a manager named Ms. Porter was responsible for hiring new staff. He spoke with Ms. Porter who told Kevin that the store was not currently hiring. Kevin called every week for a month and spoke with Ms. Porter. Each time he called, he asked if the status had changed concerning the hiring of any new staff. And each time, Ms. Porter would tell Kevin that they still weren't hiring. But one day, Kevin called and Ms. Porter said, "I'm going to put you on the payroll, but it's only going to be for a couple of hours a week, unless other employees call off, then you can take their hours." Kevin's diligence had paid off. During Kevin's employment at this store, he never worked less than 40 hours a week.

The path that is well traveled is not the path that should always be taken. Sometimes God's way is the tight path that many can't travel. Listen and hear His voice when He speaks, then you will know which way to travel. God's counsel is the counsel that will stand. His way is the way that will stand. Through any storm, His light will always shine bright to eliminate any darkness.

PROVERBS 1:5

A wise man will hear, and will increase learning;
and a man of understanding shall attain unto wise counsels:

SPECIAL DELIVERIES

Be aware of what packages you receive.
Packages are thoughts, if you sign, you receive.
Thoughts meditated upon turn into what you believe.
Once a belief takes root, it develops into a stronghold.
A personality is then formed of this stronghold like a mold.

Tim was born in an environment of lack. His family was always in need of various things. His family almost never ate out for dinner. They had rats and roaches inside their home. They had break-ins into their home. And the path Tim traveled daily to get home from school was riddled with grown men or scavengers --they attempted to steal whatever they could from Tim and his peers.

On Christmas, Tim usually received necessities such as socks or underwear, which he was very grateful for! In their cupboards were basic foods; seldom did he have delicacies such as grapes, mainly just red apples, if any fruit at all. Whenever Tim did receive the delicacies, he would savor them. Many promises were made to Tim by his father that never came to pass. Not receiving these things caused fear and doubts to set up in his mind. Tim began to hoard when he did receive good things. Tim was unaware that his thought processes were against the principles of God. Tim would remain in lack until his thought process would change. Once he grabbed ahold of God's principle of giving by faith, he believed he would get more, so he gave and gave and gave. Tim always had all his needs met.

If you want to believe God for anything, don't wait until what you believe shows up to believe. Believe you have it now! Don't look at where you are. Look forward to what you are believing God for! Watch who and what you listen to, because it can develop into what you believe – or your belief system. Listening to the wrong things can develop a wrong belief system. It's a lot easier to catch wrong thought patterns at a young age, than to attempt to break them at an older age. God's system is about giving, not hoarding! Test God's Word and give and watch Him prove His Word is true!

PROVERBS 11:24 (THE MESSAGE)

The world of the generous gets larger and larger;
the world of the stingy gets smaller and smaller.

SEEK iT OUT!

The mind that says," It's me against the world,"
will always lose.
You hurt yourself when other's advice you refuse.
Sit at the feet of the elders, listen to discern,
the wisdom in their heart is there for you to learn.

Lewis fathered two children. His two boys were as different as night and day. His son Bryce rebelled against everything his father said. His oldest son Brandon would listen and take heed to what his father said. Bryce would find his path to be rough as he grew older, he still refused to take advice and receive counsel from others.

But Brandon would find success on his life path. After marrying his wife, he was trying to decide on purchasing a home to start a family. He called his dad and explained to him that he was thinking of purchasing a home, and that he could afford to pay $120,000. He wanted to know from his dad if he should purchase a house for that amount. Lewis responded, "If your wife no longer worked, would you be able to afford the house on your salary alone?" His dad also stated, "Don't include your wife's income when deciding how much to pay for a new home." His son Brandon listened to his dad's counsel and never had to learn this valuable lesson the hard way. His son saved a lot of money by seeking counsel, and didn't get in over his head early in his marriage.

Always seek counsel when making decisions. Only a fool thinks he has all the answers to everything. Learn from those who have come up before you. Only a fool has to learn everything the hard way! When you have questions about any issue, try to run it by at least three people whom you trust to speak into your life. Once you have heard their opinions on the matter and prayed to God, then make your decision.

PROVERBS 20:18 (AMPLIFIED BIBLE)

Purposes and plans are established by counsel;

STICK WITH THE DETAILS

Sometimes instructions are barked with a
tone that's border line rude.
The lesson is still there, even though the bark
has changed your whole mood.
Think of the growth before you become offended.
Don't take it personal; your feelings can easily be mended.

Lamont was the starting point guard on his college basketball team. He learned a valuable lesson during one of his games. His team was down three points and as Lamont dribbled the basketball across half court, his coach called for a time out. The team huddled around their coach for instructions. Their coach began to draw up a play for the team to run, within the eight seconds they had left. The coach wanted Lamont to dribble the basketball to the left side of the floor. Their shooting guard Mike was supposed to run the baseline through two screens set for him and sprint up the lane, where he would use a double screen to get open for a three-pointer to tie the game. But as the team broke from the huddle, the shooting guard, Mike, angry because the coach had told him earlier in the game to pick his spots when shooting the ball, emphatically stated, "I'm not shooting the ball!" Lamont pled with Mike to follow the play their coach had drawn up, but Mike continued to express that he would not shoot the ball.

Lamont thought Mike was just bluffing and that he would follow through with the play and shoot the ball. He was their best three point shooter! As Lamont called out the play with the clock ticking, Mike stood on the baseline with his hands on his hips. Lamont knew then that Mike was serious about not shooting the ball. And as the time wound down five, four, three, two, and one, Lamont made a quick move and shot a three pointer. The ball didn't even touch the rim as the time expired! The team lost the game. The next day at practice, Lamont's coach lined up everyone on the baseline. He paced back and forth screaming, "When I set up a play, that means that play should be run!" The coach had everyone start running sprints, and that's what they did for the remainder of practice. Lamont took the coaches chastisement without ever mentioning what Mike had done.

Paying attention to detail is extremely important in every part of life. It takes practice to pay attention to detail. Small details can make big changes. Missing small details can lead to death in some situations. When receiving instructions, make sure you're clear before separating from the source. Ask questions, even at the point of sounding or appearing foolish. Take notes, if you find it necessary to do so!

PROVERBS 4:13 (AMPLIFIED BIBLE)

Take firm hold of instruction, do not let go;
guard her, for she is your life.

YOUR HEART IS THE PRIZE

Fill your heart with God and His commands.
Others may seek to steal your heart, but don't
give in to their demands.
Your well being lies in a healthy heart.
Only allow God in that space is how you do your part.

While away at school in California, Dale was focused on getting an education and playing basketball. But he had a girlfriend back in his home town, almost 3,000 miles away. He loved this girlfriend with all his heart. About one month into his stay in California, Dale found out that his girlfriend had cheated on him with another guy. Dale's heart was so wrapped up in his girlfriend, he started to lose focus on why he was in school in California. He attempted to call her constantly. It took a ten dollar roll of quarters to talk to her for less than five minutes. He spent most of his money he had saved calling his girlfriend at a nearby telephone booth. Dale's schoolwork and basketball training suffered, due to his broken heart. Things in California began to head downward for Dale. Eventually, the electricity in his apartment was turned off and he was behind several months on his lease payment. Down to his last $150.00, Dale purchased a bus ticket and took the three day bus ride back to his hometown. His heart wouldn't be happy until he made his way back to his hometown to talk face to face with his girlfriend. Amidst many attempts at reconciliation, upon Dale's return home, he wasn't able to reconcile his relationship with his girlfriend. Her heart was with the other man! Dale's heart, wrapped up in his girlfriend, had led him to drop out of school and leave a basketball scholarship behind.

Your strength lies with what or who has your heart. Don't ever give your strength to a woman! Stay focused on your life's mission. Whatever God has put in your heart, do it with all your heart. Females can wait. Finish your schooling and find your purpose. Get established first before even thinking of settling down or falling for a woman. And get to know a woman thoroughly before you get emotionally attached. Never get to the point of no return before you do a thorough check of a female.

PROVERBS 4:23 (NEW LIVING TRANSLATION)
Guard your heart above all else, for it
determines the course of your life.

A MAN THAT FINDS A GOOD WIFE FINDS A GOOD THING

It's very important who you choose for your wife
The choice you make will have a great impact on your life.
The mother of your children is a key role she will hold.
A friend and partner, you'll hang out together as you grow old.

Below is a list of qualifications you should consider when choosing a wife. It is an excerpt taken from The Message Bible, of the 31st chapter of Proverbs verses 10 through 31:

Hymn to a Good Wife
"A good woman is hard to find, and worth far more than diamonds. Her husband trusts her without reserve' and never has reason to regret it. Never spiteful, she treats him generously all her life long. She shops around for the best yarns and cottons, and enjoys knitting and sewing. She's like a trading ship that sails to faraway places and brings back exotic surprises. She's up before dawn, preparing breakfast for her family and organizing her day. She looks over a field and buys it, then, with money she's put aside, plants a garden. First thing in the morning, she dresses for work, rolls up her sleeves, eager to get started. She senses the worth of her work, is in no hurry to call it quits for the day. She's skilled in the crafts of home and hearth, diligent in homemaking. She's quick to assist anyone in need, reaches out to help the poor. She doesn't worry about her family when it snows; their winter clothes are all mended and ready to wear. She makes her own clothing, and dresses in colorful linens and silks. Her husband is greatly respected when he deliberates with the city fathers. She designs gowns and sells them, brings the sweater she knits to the dress shop. Her clothes are well made and elegant, and she always faces tomorrow with a smile. When she speaks she has something worthwhile to say, and she always says it kindly. She keeps an eye on everyone in her household, and keeps them all busy and productive. Her children respect and bless her; her husband joins in with words of praise: Many women have done wonderful things, but you've outclassed them all! Charm can mislead and beauty soon fades. The woman to be admired and praised is the woman who lives in the Fear-of-God. Give her everything she deserves! Festoon her life with praises!"

KNOW WHERE YOUR CHEDDAR IS GOING

Get trained so you can earn enough to pay bills.
When you're living with parents, you have no worries;
your money is spent on thrills.
Always know where your money is going.
Live on a budget; you'll find your money is growing.

Marvin dropped out of High School before he completed his sophomore year. Although his parents pled with him to stay in school, he felt school just wasn't worth it and refused to go back. He found a job that paid $10.00 an hour. He worked forty hours a week, lived at his parent's home, and felt he was doing well. He moved into his own apartment. Below is a chart describing his current living expenses:

Marvin brings home $1,600 a month before taxes.

Tithes	$160
Rent	$500
Food	$200
Car Insurance	$200
Fuel	$200
Renter's Insurance	$100
Cell Phone	$60
Heat	$60
Lights	$30
	———
	$1,510 (Total)

Get trained and continue to get training! When you have no skills, you are left to the mercy of those who decide to hire you. Training gives you options in what kinds of employment you can choose from. You see in the above illustration that Marvin had no skills or training and the job he had didn't provide him with enough money to pay his bills. And this list excludes cable TV, clothing, or money for a date. Let Marvin's story be motivation to keep you in school! When the Lord blesses you, He will not add any drama with it, no struggles!

The blessing of the Lord makes a person rich,
and he adds no sorrow with it.

WHEN YOU STEP OUT OF BED

To live with purpose gives you energy,
much more than working for someone for a nominal fee.
Find what you love and set that trail ablaze.
Set your focus as a compass, determined to
see your vision through life's maze.

Caleb grabbed a lighter and a hack saw. He then took a blue milk crate, turned it upside down and began to burn and saw the bottom out of the crate. He took the crate and nailed it to a square piece of wood. He nailed the square wood with the milk crate onto a tree in front of his house. Caleb and his friends played basketball on this make shift basketball hoop night and day throughout the summer. Caleb was twelve years old and had decided that he would make it to the NBA. Everyday Caleb stepped from his bed, he had the thought of making it to the NBA on his mind. As Caleb played basketball outside, his Mom called him inside several times a day to go to the store. Caleb walked to the store with his basketball dribbling with his right hand on the way to the store, and on the way home from the store dribbling with his left hand. He worked on his handles constantly. After the night covered the day, Caleb went inside to watch basketball on TV. While watching a basketball game, during each commercial, Caleb would do pushups on his finger tips. Caleb read books to increase his reading comprehension as a way to keep his schooling and basketball up to pace – he realized that his school had to be kept up in order for him to play basketball.

He played for a fundamentally sound little league coach and went on to play on a very competitive inner city high school team. Caleb sought out basketball camps to attend, but could not afford to attend any of the top camps. He went on to college and played on a basketball scholarship. During the summer, he would work and save the change from any dollar bill that was broken for his laundry money during the school year. While working a summer job at a fast food restaurant, his focus was always on school and the NBA, so when customers would mean mug him, it didn't matter because he knew the job was temporary. He completed his college playing career and received his degree. He tried out at an overseas basketball camp, but didn't latch on with any of the teams. He didn't make it to the NBA, but he did get all of his college education paid for.

Caleb lived in a world full of fun experiences during his playing career and his vision kept him off of the wrong path. Always live with purpose! Have something to shoot for; don't just go with the flow! Live on purpose! Shoot for the stars – if you miss, you still land higher than you started!

PROVERBS 16:9 (THE MESSAGE)

We plan the way we want to live, but only God makes us able to live it.

STAY BUSY

Idleness is the devil's workshop.
Laziness is a habit one should not adopt.
It will fly under the radar and when you least suspect,
nab you of ambition and leave you unable to protect.

James was playing touch football on his block one summer day. Playing quarterback, he hiked the football, and the defensive player began counting one dog, two dog, three dog…! James looked and looked for a receiver to throw the ball to, and as soon as the defensive player reached seven dog on his count, he rushed in to tag James. As James jumped in the air to throw the football, the defensive player pushed him to the ground. In an attempt to break his fall, both of James' hands hit the ground first. When James was helped up from the ground, he heard his wrist pop. James continued playing football for a little while longer until he looked and both wrists were swollen. Afraid to go home at first, he finally went home. He didn't immediately tell his mom – he fell asleep. After a brief nap, James woke up in pain and finally showed his mom the massive swelling on both his wrist. His mom took him to the hospital immediately! Armed with two casts, one for each of his arms, James returned to school. He couldn't write, so he would receive a library pass daily. His grades began to drop. He lost the desire to work hard at his grades. Any time James didn't want to complete an assignment, he would use his wrist injuries as an excuse to get out of completing his work. He developed a lazy work ethic that he would carry into his first two years of high school. Eventually, his desire to excel in school did return.

Laziness will destroy lives! Visions or dreams will never be fulfilled as long as laziness is present. Whenever the hint of laziness is present, break it immediately with some sort of hard work, or by doing some undesirable task.

PROVERBS 18:9 (THE MESSAGE)
Slack habits and sloppy work are as bad as vandalism.

"ASK"

Decisions will be made in abundance.
The child next door may be the one God sends, not a prince,
to give you the answers you seek.
Receive the people God sends with a heart that's meek.

Lisa and Romeo, a young married couple, have learned some valuable lessons about seeking counsel on making big purchases or major decisions. Most of the decisions they've made have been backed by the counsel they sought, and being led by God. These decisions had led to the blessing of God being poured into their lives. But, on the other hand, some of the decisions they've made have led to losses.

Let's take a look and learn from the mistakes they made. Romeo received a package in the mail with an ignition key inside. The advertisement stated that if the ignition key received in the mail fit inside an ignition of one of the cars at their dealership, you win the car. Romeo made his way to the dealership. The key he possessed was inserted, but did not fit. Elizabeth, a salesperson at the dealership, immediately began to sell Romeo on the large selection of used cars the dealership had to offer. Romeo wasn't in the market to purchase a new vehicle, but he listened and began to consider what she was saying. Without seeking counsel or hearing from God, Romeo bought a used car from the dealership.

Another occasion counsel was not sought was when Lisa and Romeo walked into a new fitness center that opened in their neighborhood. The salesperson walked them both through the entire place, pointing out all the benefits of the fitness center, then explained that they offered the services of a personal trainer. This added fee was a lot more that would be paid monthly in addition to the regular membership fee. As Lisa and Romeo sat in front of the salesperson, he pushed for the personal trainer. Romeo vehemently rejected the idea of the personal trainer, but was unable to convince his wife. She had become entranced with the salesperson's pitch for the personal trainer. She decided without her husband's counsel or hearing from God that she would pay the money for the personal trainer. Later on, Lisa realized that she had made a mistake in signing up for the personal trainer.

Always seek counsel before making major decisions. If possible, try to obtain counsel from at least three credible people and allow God to lead you, before making any final decisions. There are traps set that seek to steal your money, kill you, and destroy all the plans God has for you to prosper in life. God has placed people in your life that He will speak through to get His message to you.

The way of a fool is right in his own eyes,
but he who listens to counsel is wise.

KEEP IT MOVING

Sometimes things won't go as you plan.
Nevertheless, don't get caught spectating;
you're a gamer, not a fan.
Suck it up, even if a turnover is made.
You only get credit for the minutes you've played.

Lawrence was miserable working at a paper plant, since he had made the decision to leave school and give up his dream of playing basketball on a basketball scholarship. Lawrence had been working full time at the paper company, and had saved enough money to purchase a used car with his earnings. One day, a former teammate from his high school called him and offered him a proposition. His teammate said, "An assistant coach from my school is taking a head coaching position at a college in your area; do you still want to play basketball?" Lawrence, overfilled with joy, emphatically said, "Yes!" Lawrence gave the paper company two weeks' notice of his resignation. About a month later, Lawrence drove to the college where his basketball skills were on display in front of the coaching staff. After the try out ended, Lawrence was offered a full basketball scholarship. As the summer came to an end, the first day of school was approaching quickly. Lawrence learned that he would be living with a teammate in a place directly across from the college. Lawrence wouldn't be able to move into his place until the first day of school. The night before the first day of school, at about 2:00am, Lawrence had completed packing his things in his car – in what he thought was secret and darkness of the night. He finally dozed off to sleep, but was awakened a couple of hours later to his mom's startling statement, "Lawrence, did you leave your sunroof off?" Lawrence knew he hadn't left his sunroof off, and as he opened the front door, he saw all of the belongings that were packed inside his car scattered across his lawn. Thieves had stolen his valuables and thrown his clothes across the lawn. Although very upset, Lawrence had to repack the clothes that remained and head to school.

In life, there is no time to dwell on past miseries. Pack up your things and get moving! If you've just left a place that wasn't a good place, don't revisit it again! Life doesn't stand still. It keeps on moving. Whether you complete your college degree in five years or you decide not to go to school, time will move on anyhow.

PROVERBS 4:25 (THE MESSAGE)
Keep your eyes straight ahead; ignore all sideshow distractions.

THE BIRDS AND THE BEES

Between a man and his mate
lies the power to procreate.
When the pair becomes one
exemplifies God's definition of married couple having fun.

Byron's son Dwayne is nine years old. While watching television, Byron notices that there are many sexual references being made. Byron is concerned because he hasn't talked to his son about the birds and the bees. He had previously attempted a conversation about sex about one year ago, but his son kind of blew it off. Byron knew that his son was being exposed to many different messages about sex. One day, Byron sat Dwayne down to have this conversation about the birds and the bees.

This is what God told him to say. God only permits sex between a man and a woman within a marriage union, and that a husband should always buy his wife flowers, and not just on special occasions. A husband should listen to his wife and find out what she likes and dislikes. He should open doors and pull out her chair before she sits down. Compliment her with words that build her up. Hold her hand when out in public. Hug her and passionately kiss her whenever the opportunity arises. A husband should always seek to fulfill her needs above his own needs. And when special occasions come around, a husband should go all out with the gifts he purchases. Study his wife to find out what her interests are at the time of these special occasions, and purchase gifts based off of these interests. Remain faithful to her! And stay satisfied with her bosom!

Just know that once God leads you to the woman you should marry, cherish this woman as the gift God has given you. And after you two have had the opportunity to enjoy one another for some time, an arrangement by God will be made for your sperm to fertilize the egg that lies within your wife. Once this happens, your bundle of joy will be born!

PROVERBS 18:22 (AMPLIFIED BIBLE)

He who finds a [true] wife finds a good thing
and obtains favor from the Lord.

CONCLUSION

In Proverbs 8:12, 14-36 (NLT), listen to the heartbeat of wisdom.

"I, Wisdom, live together with good judgment.
　I know where to discover knowledge and discernment.

Common sense and success belong to me.
　Insight and strength are mine.
Because of me, kings reign,
　and rulers make just decrees.
Rulers lead with my help,
　and nobles make righteous judgments.
"I love all who love me.
　Those who search will surely find me.
I have riches and honor,
　as well as enduring wealth and justice.
My gifts are better than gold, even the purest gold,
　my wages better than sterling silver!
I walk in righteousness,
　in paths of justice.
Those who love me inherit wealth.
　I will fill their treasuries.
"The Lord formed me from the beginning,
　before he created anything else.
I was appointed in ages past,
　at the very first, before the earth began.
I was born before the oceans were created,
　before the springs bubbled forth their waters.
Before the mountains were formed,
　before the hills, I was born—
before he had made the earth and fields
　and the first handfuls of soil.
I was there when he established the heavens,
　when he drew the horizon on the oceans.
I was there when he set the clouds above,
　when he established springs deep in the earth.
I was there when he set the limits of the seas,
　so they would not spread beyond their boundaries.

And when he marked off the earth's foundations,
    I was the architect at his side.
I was his constant delight,
    rejoicing always in his presence.
And how happy I was with the world he created;
    how I rejoiced with the human family!
"And so, my children, listen to me,
    for all who follow my ways are joyful.
Listen to my instruction and be wise.
    Don't ignore it.
Joyful are those who listen to me,
    watching for me daily at my gates,
    waiting for me outside my home!
For whoever finds me finds life
    and receives favor from the Lord.
But those who miss me injure themselves.
    All who hate me love death."

Wisdom already knows what you are attempting to figure out! Just seek wisdom; she has the answers you desire! She has the answers for whatever questions you pose!

IF YOU'RE A FAN OF THIS BOOK, PLEASE TELL OTHERS...

- Write about *Straight Up!* on your blog, Twitter, MySpace, and Facebook page.
- Suggest *Straight Up!* to friends.
- When you're in a bookstore, ask them if they carry the book. The book is available through all major distributors, so any bookstore that does not have *Straight Up!* in stock can easily order it.
- Write a positive review of *Straight Up!* on www.amazon.com.
- Send my publisher, HigherLife Publishing, suggestions on Web sites, conferences, and events you know of where this book could be offered at media@ahigherlife.com.
- Purchase additional copies to give away as gifts.

CONNECT WITH ME...

To learn more about *Straight Up!*, please contact me at:
Michael Davis
straightuptogod@gmail.com

You may also contact my publisher directly:
HigherLife Publishing
400 Fontana Circle
Building 1 – Suite 105
Oviedo, Florida 32765
Phone: (407) 563-4806
Email: media@ahigherlife.com